moments of
MINDFULNESS

ESME FIELDING

summersdale

MOMENTS OF MINDFULNESS

Summersdale Publishers Ltd
46 West Street
Chichester
West Sussex
PO19 1RP
UK

www.summersdale.com

Printed and bound in China

ISBN: 978-1-84953-406-2

Substantial discounts on bulk quantities of Summersdale books are available to corporations, professional associations and other organisations. For details contact Nicky Douglas by telephone: +44 (0) 1243 756902, fax: +44 (0) 1243 786300, or email: nicky@summersdale.com.

INTRODUCTION

Mindfulness is about being aware of the present moment, without judgement or worry for the past or the future, calmly and peacefully. It allows you to experience the magic and wonder in this life that we have, and to listen to the wisdom of your own heart. Let this book guide you from morning to night, showing how you can bring small but beautiful moments of mindfulness to each and every day.

Be especially aware of your

JUDGEMENTS

and expectations today.

LET GO OF

the stress of perfectionism.

On waking, spend some moments

BECOMING AWARE

of your body, listening to the

SOUNDS

around you and

NOTICING

what thoughts are in your mind.

Say these words quietly to yourself throughout today:

'I AM A BEING OF PEACE.'

Find a few minutes in your morning routine

TO SIT QUIETLY

and greet the day ahead.

INSTEAD OF RUSHING

straight into your day's activities.

Have a

NO-RUSH ATTITUDE

to your work today. This means

DOING THINGS THOROUGHLY

and with less stress.

Before you begin any journey today,

TAKE A MOMENT

to centre yourself and

SET OFF WITH HAPPINESS

and a sense of well-being.

Take a moment today to

FOCUS ON YOUR BREATHING.

It relaxes the space inside of you,

STRAIGHTENS YOUR SPINE,

opens the chest and expands your heart.

Open all the windows around you.

FEEL THE BREEZE

on your skin and

SMELL THE FRESH AIR.

As you go about your day,

SEND SILENT MESSAGES OF LOVE

to those around you,

WHETHER THEY ARE STRANGERS

or old friends.

Stand under a tree and
ENJOY THE SOUNDS
of leaves gently rustling and
THE SIGHT OF GREENS
and browns in harmony.

BE ESPECIALLY MINDFUL
of the words you use today.

SPEAK FROM A PLACE
of love.

Place water outside

FOR THE BIRDS –

and take a moment

TO WATCH THEM

wash and preen their feathers.

Focus on an

OBJECT FROM NATURE

such as a flower or a seashell.

SEE ITS BEAUTY AND INTRICACY,

and place all other thoughts to one side

WHILE YOU MARVEL AT THE DETAIL

of this natural object.

If something difficult happens today,

NOTICE WHICH PARTS
of your body feel tense, then

BREATHE INTO THE AREA
to help you relax.

Close your eyes and

LISTEN MINDFULLY

for one minute today to all the

SOUNDS AROUND YOU.

For one minute, you have

NOTHING ELSE TO DO.

Just listen.

Incense or aromatherapy oils

ARE LOVELY TO BURN.

They clear your surroundings of sluggish air.

BREATHE SLOWLY AND ENJOY

the cleansing aromas.

When your mind starts to flag,

CHANGE YOUR ENERGY

by moving your body:

STRETCH, TAKE A WALK

or get a drink.

Walk barefoot on grass –

THE EARTH IS A GREAT RECYCLER

of negative energy, so allow all

THE STRESSES OF YOUR LIFE

to flow through your feet and

INTO THE EARTH.

All words contain

ENERGY AND VIBRATION;

therefore, transform your inner critic to

A VOICE OF KINDNESS

and love.

When our minds are

ENGULFED WITH STORIES

of our past or future,

WE ARE MISSING

the experience of the moment.

TODAY, KEEP REMEMBERING

the moments you are in.

Hidden in the word 'listen'

IS THE WORD 'SILENT'

Choose to make a conscious effort to

SWITCH OFF THE NOISE

around you, and allow the silence

TO FILL YOUR MIND.

Be aware of phrases

YOU OFTEN REPEAT

throughout the day – some of these

MAY BE PART

of a negative pattern.

BE KINDER TO YOURSELF.

CLOUD-WATCH.
Allow the gentle movements
ACROSS THE SKY
to fill you with
TRANQUILLITY AND CALM.

Become conscious of your breath
AND VISUALISE IT
filling the whole of your body.
A FEW MOMENTS
of this awareness and you will feel
LIGHTER AND BRIGHTER.

We all rush from one place to another –
SLOW DOWN
with mindful walking.
TAKE SLOWER BREATHS,
feel your feet touching the ground,
AND BRING AWARENESS
to your body as it moves.

Celebrate today's successes and

ACHIEVEMENTS.

Encourage and

PRAISE YOURSELF

before dashing on to

NEW CHALLENGES..

Work slowly and deliberately on

ONE TASK AT A TIME.

Keep your mind

ON THE PRESENT,

not the past or the future.

For a whole day, think and say

POSITIVE THINGS.

Hold back on negative or sarcastic comments.

LAUGH AT YOURSELF

when you discover how much negativity

YOU CARRY IN YOUR MIND.

Imagine that

WITHIN YOUR HEART

you carry around a lighted candle.

SEE OTHERS TOO,

with their flames glowing. Appreciate the

LIGHT IN EVERYONE!

Today, accept things

AS THEY HAPPEN

and accept people for

WHO THEY ARE,

including yourself.

Don't miss an opportunity today to

WATCH THE WIND

gusting through the trees and

WHIRLING DOWN THE STREET.

Notice how nature touches everything.

Arrange flowers in a vase,

PAYING ATTENTION

to their beauty,

TEXTURE AND SCENT.

IF YOU FIND YOURSELF

dwelling on negative or anxious thoughts,

BRING TO MIND

a beautiful image and

ALLOW YOURSELF

to be soothed.

If you usually avoid walking in the rain, don't!

A WALK IN THE RAIN

can bring another dimension

TO YOUR SURROUNDINGS

and there can be a heightened

SENSE OF SMELL,

sound and feeling.

Carry lavender oil with you so that you

CAN REFRESH YOURSELF

and your space wherever you are.

THE OIL CAN BE RUBBED

onto pulse points to aid relaxation and

CREATE A SENSE OF CALM.

Repeat this affirmation

QUIETLY TO YOURSELF

as you go about your day:

'I AM RELAXED.'

Take a moment to

'BELLY BREATHE'

for a greater flow of oxygen and instant calm

BREATHE IN DEEPLY,

allowing your stomach to rise outwards.

ON THE OUT BREATH,

allow your stomach to fall back.

FIND SOME WATER

where you can calmly reflect –

A RIVER, THE SEA OR A LAKE

or even a town square fountain.

Light a candle and

REFLECT ON HOW

it brings illumination

TO THE DARKNESS,

just as you can radiate brightly today

IN ALL YOU DO.

Today, inside and out.

NOTICE THE SUNLIGHT.

It can stream in through your window or

DAZZLE YOU

from between the clouds.

ABSORB IT

and luxuriate in its warmth.

Notice when you are

JUDGING THINGS

as good or bad.

PAUSE.

Tell yourself there doesn't need to be good or bad:

LIFE HAPPENS.

Feel light and free.

Imagine you are

CULTIVATING WISDOM

wherever you go and in

WHATEVER YOU DO

by being at peace.

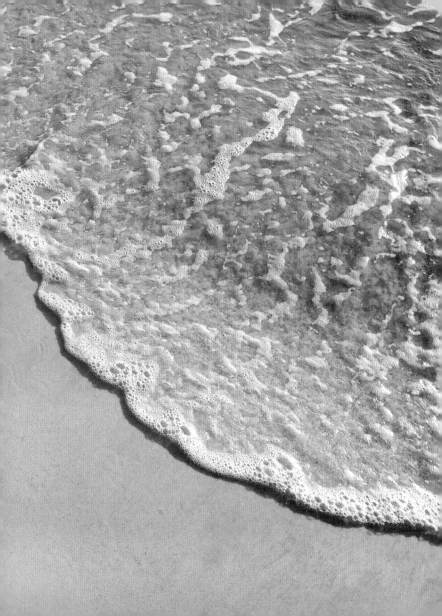

Try to find a

WIDE HORIZON

from a hilltop and let your eyes

LOSE FOCUS

into the distance.

THE LACK OF SHARP FOCUS

is very calming.

While eating your meal,

FOCUS ALL YOUR ATTENTION

on eating, placing your fork down

IN BETWEEN MOUTHFULS

to take time while chewing.

SAVOUR EACH

mouthful and bring awareness to every taste.

Have a luxurious bath,

BEING MINDFUL

of all your senses.

ENJOY THE WARM WATER,

the bath oils, scented candles,

FLUFFY TOWELS

and relaxing music.

Before you go to bed tonight,

SPEND A MINUTE

breathing out the negative experiences

OF THE DAY,

and breathing in serenity and calm

BEFORE YOU LIE

down to sleep.

If you're interested in finding out more about our books,
find us on Facebook at Summersdale Publishers
and follow us on Twitter at @Summersdale.

www.summersdale.com